Play With Shapes!

Joyce Markovics

rourkeeducationalmedia.com

Teacher Notes available at
rem4teachers.com

www.rourkeeducationalmedia.com

PHOTO CREDITS: Cover: © ; Title Page: © Sandra Cunningham; Page 3: © AlbanyPictures; Page 4: © Sandra Van Der Steen, © IvonneW; Page 5: © kaisphoto; Page 6, 7: © Mikalai Bachkou; Page 8: © Denis And Yulia Pogostins; Page 9, 11, 15, 17: © Andrija Markovic; Page 10: © John Siebert; Page 12, 13: Laser143; Page 14, 16: © Dan Klimke; Page 18: © rraheb; Page 20: © Cheryl Casey; Page 21: © FlamingPumpkin; Page 22: © mbbirdy, © Ghenadii Boico; Page 23: © Anton Balazh, © Ivan Gusev, © Laindiapiaroa

Edited by Precious McKenzie
Cover and Interior page design by Teri Intzegian

Library of Congress PCN Data

Play With Shapes! / Joyce Markovics
(Little World Math Concepts)
ISBN 978-1-61810-078-8 (hard cover)(alk. paper)
ISBN 978-1-61810-211-9 (soft cover)
Library of Congress Control Number: 2011944388

Rourke Educational Media
Printed in the United States of America,
North Mankato, Minnesota

rourkeeducationalmedia.com

customerservice@rourkeeducationalmedia.com • PO Box 643328 Vero Beach, Florida 32964

Grab a shovel and pail! Let's explore solid shapes at the seashore.

Did you know that everything has a shape or form?

Trace around the starfish with your finger. The outline of the starfish is its shape.

There are many different shapes at the shore. Take a look.

What shapes do you see?

Here comes a beach ball! What solid shape is it? The beach ball is a sphere

A sphere is round all over.

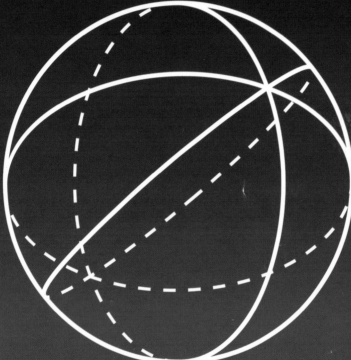

SPHERE

What else do you know that is round like a sphere?

What shape is this piece of ice? The ice has a cube shape.

A cube has six sides. Each side is the same length.

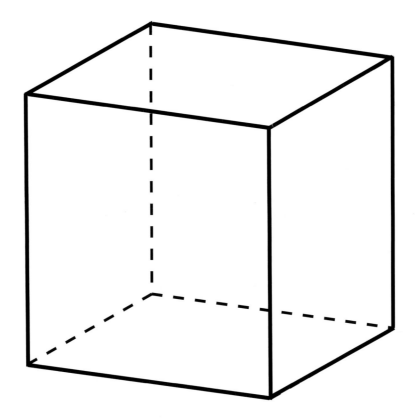

CUBE

What are some other solid shapes at the beach?

Let's find out by playing with sand.

What solid shape is the top
of the sandcastle? The top
of the sandcastle is a cone.

CONE ⟶

A cone has a round bottom and a point at the top.

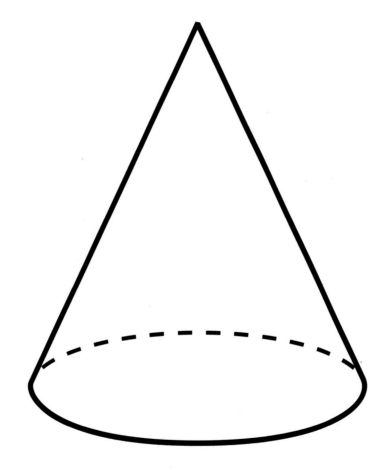

CONE

Below the cone shape is a cylinder.

CYLINDER ⟶

A cylinder is shaped like a tube.

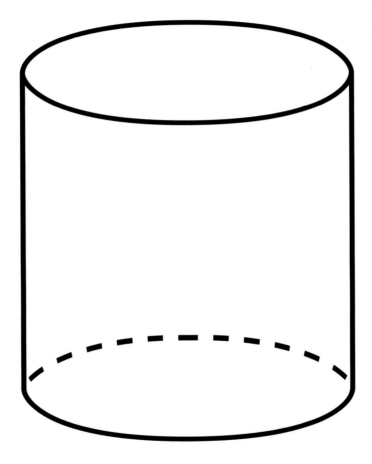

CYLINDER

See the shape of the sand pile?
The sand has a pyramid shape.

A pyramid has a square bottom and a point at the top.

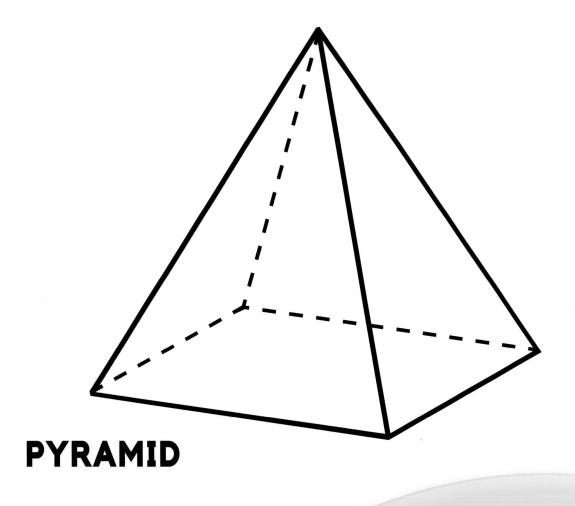

PYRAMID

Let's dig in the sand for seashells!

What can you find?

Point out all the shapes and solids you see at the seashore.

Shapes and solids are up, down, and all around!

Index

Websites

www.pbskids.org/games/shapes.html

www.nickjr.com/games/all-shows/numbers-shapes/all-ages/
index.jhtml

www.nga.gov/kids/zone/zone.htm

About the Author

Joyce Markovics is a writer and editor. She shares her home in New York City with her husband, Adam, and a menagerie of pets that includes a spirited house rabbit named Pearl and a crooning frog. She has written over 15 books and enjoys thinking and writing about abstract concepts for young readers.

Ask The Author!
www.rem4students.com